ILLUSTRATED IN COLOR

A WAY OF SEEING

THE INWARD & OUTWARD VISION OF LILIAS TROTTER

WATERCOLORS SELECTED FROM THE OXLEY COLLECTION OF EGERTON/TROTTER ARCHIVES
(JOURNALS & SKETCHBOOKS) QUOTATIONS FROM THE WRITINGS OF LILIAS TROTTER

ARTIST & AUTHOR: LILIAS TROTTER

EDITED & COMPILED BY: MIRIAM HUFFMAN ROCKNESS

PUBLISHED BY

OXVISION
BOOKS

ACKNOWLEDGMENTS

We gratefully acknowledge those involved in the preservation and publication of the Oxley Collection of the Egerton/Trotter Archives: Hugh and Claire Egerton; Alexander Egerton; Alasdair McLaren; Lilias Trotter Advisory Board: Carol Holquist, Marjorie Lampe Mead, Sally Oxley, Bonnie Palmquist, Miriam Rockness; Brian Oxley.

ISBN **978 1 938068 19 5**

Library of Congress Control Number: 2016944733

Published by Oxvision Books
4001 Tamiami Trail North, Suite 250, Naples, FL 34103

Find us at: **liliastrotter.com   oxvisionmedia.com   oxvisionfilms.com**

Dedicated to the Life and Legacy of Lilias Trotter who continues to teach us to see with heart-sight as well as eyesight.

A Way of Seeing: The Inward & Outward Vision of Lilias Trotter

This book is part of a special collection of Oxvision projects highlighting Lilias Trotter. Our challenge is to bring Lilias to life through her art, her writings, her sacrifice and her incredible story. To that end we have produced a major documentary, *Many Beautiful Things*, to tell her story with the rich narrative it deserves. We have also painstakingly reproduced two of her beautiful sketchbooks in facsimile editions: her *1876 Sketchbook: Scenes from Lucerne to Venice* and her *1889 Sketchbook: Scenes of North Africa, Italy & Switzerland*. Also, from Lilias Trotter's brush and pen we offer a facsimile edition of her devotional classic *Parables of the Cross* and now *A Way of Seeing*. Finally, we offer a picture book with special appeal to "children of all ages," *Lily: The Girl Who Could See*, beautifully illustrated by Tim Ladwig. You can learn more about this amazing woman and our accompanying products by visiting us online at **liliastrotter.com.**

A Haunting Care: John Ruskin and Lilias Trotter

During a visit to Venice in 1876, the mother of twenty-three-year-old Lilias Trotter heard that John Ruskin, then fifty-seven, was in the city to work on drawings and to revise his book of 1851-53, *The Stones of Venice*. Carefully drafting a letter of introduction, she must have hoped that Lilias might receive some instruction in drawing or at least some general commendation from the foremost writer on art of his day. Probably she was expecting no more than that, although there would have been the obvious excitement of personal contact with one of the most famous people in the English-speaking world. Having given "somewhat sulky permission," Ruskin was surprised to see "extremely rightminded and careful work," and asked "that the young lady might be allowed to come out sketching with me." "She seemed to learn everything the instant she was shown it," he recalled, "and ever so much more than she was taught."

It is well known that Ruskin had an eye for young women of intelligence, dedication, of good Christian upbringing, and with a talent for art. These virtues lie at the heart of *Sesame and Lilies* (1865), a hugely popular book—undoubtedly known to the Trotters—which had lasting influence in support of women's education. *Ethics of the Dust*, which followed in 1866, derived in part from the tuition in drawing which Ruskin had given to the girls of Winnington School near Northwich, Cheshire, where he was a patron and regular visitor between 1859 and 1868. Later correspondence with some of the girls in adult life still centered on the improvement of their draughtsmanship but also provided a kind of surrogate family for an only child with few close relatives of his own and whose ill-fated and unconsummated marriage had been annulled long before.

Having seen from examples of her drawing that she was worth encouraging, he added Lilias to his group of protégées, alongside most recently Louise Blandy, who received drawing lessons in London in 1875, and Amy Yule, whom he had visited in Palermo in 1874. A sketchbook survives from 1876 whose later sheets show evidence of Lilias adding studies of both Gothic architecture and plants—exactly what would have been recommended by Ruskin. Earlier pages demonstrate considerable skill in figure drawing, in pencil lightly touched with watercolor, something that held little interest for Ruskin but which became one of her strengths. When in due course she came to interweave text with her drawings—or vice versa—her style as an artist had fully matured.

Forty letters written to Lilias between 1879 and 1887—sadly, her replies have not survived—illuminate a relationship that developed beyond one of master and pupil, described by Ruskin himself as "a haunting care." She becomes "darling Lilias" by 1883; Ruskin first signs himself as "ever your loving" in 1882; and he remained her "affectionate but very sorrowful" correspondent in the last surviving letter of 1887. This was not unique in correspondence with young women, the same endearments being used of Dora Livesey, Jessie Leete, and Kathleen Olander at much the same time, but with the exception of Kate Greenaway, Lilias was rare among those he called his "pets" in having shown a genuine artistic talent. For once, Ruskin might have thought he had found someone biddable to his will, one who shared his conviction that a flower, an insect, or a landscape are all part of divine creation and could be better understood by looking, and especially by drawing (a principle that still holds good today). This common belief would have been cemented during her visits in 1879 and 1885 to Brantwood, Ruskin's home at Coniston, in the Lake District of northwest England.

Ruskin played his part in raising awareness of economic inequality (through his book of 1862, *Unto This Last*) and had offered the social reformer Octavia Hill practical and financial help in the improvement of living conditions for the poor in

London, but it is clear from the letters that he regarded Lilias's decision to devote herself increasingly to what Ruskin called "trying to do good" among "naughty people" as a distraction from her artistic development. Perhaps in an effort to make her realize how much he valued her work, he placed a number of her drawings—of figures, plants, and animals, from a sketchbook made on a trip to Norway—in the teaching collection of the drawing school he had established at Oxford University. Even thinking of calling them the "Lilias series," he described them in a letter as "simply and beyond debate, the best lesson-drawings I ever saw, and every one at Oxford feels them to be so." In public, too, he commended her work in one of his *Art of England* lectures delivered at Oxford in 1883.

The correspondence lasted until 1887, two years before Ruskin suffered a major physical and mental collapse that left him confined to Brantwood until his death in 1900, unable to write even a single line. While he would never know about Lilias's later achievements as a missionary, she dutifully continued to send him good wishes, accompanied by letters and drawings. As late as 1899 she sent him a book of religious verse, accompanied by "grateful and loving memories."

Her own publications, most famously *Parables of the Cross*, together with her manuscript diaries and sketchbooks, are distinctive and unique, evidence of a quite exceptional talent, albeit one destined never to be widely known or recognized. Possibly her greatest success had been a personal one, in changing a long-held opinion of Ruskin's. "For more than five and twenty years of my life," he declared, "I would not believe that women could paint pictures, and all of history seemed to be on the side of this conviction. But I was wrong in this established conviction of mine: women can paint!"

—*Stephen Wildman*
Professor of the History of Art, Lancaster University
Director, Ruskin Library and Research Centre

I. Lilias Trotter

(1853-1928)

This little volume, *A Way of Seeing*, is intended to be more than simply a selection of Lilias Trotter's work, presented for the viewer's enjoyment. Lilias's drawings, paintings, and sketches form a record of her visceral and almost mystical communion with the natural world, a world which she beheld as much with a quickened spiritual eye as with the trained vision of an artist. The result is a collection of colorful jewels, each capturing the very essence of the scene, the plant, the person, or the object before her eyes. Her ability to see and then artistically render the very essence, the *quiddity* of what she beheld, was singled out by her mentor and friend, the great Victorian art critic John Ruskin, when he praised her uncanny skill in making a "minute, instantaneous and unerring record of the things that are precisely best."

Very few people possess this rare artistic gift, but all of us possess, at least potentially, the ability to pay close attention to what is before our eyes, to be patient as we behold an object or scene, to linger on it long enough, tenderly and attentively enough, for it to begin to reveal its own unique nature. This was Lilias Trotter's way of seeing, and it can become yours as well. Spend time with the images, enough time to allow your spirit's inner eye to awaken, and your imagination to stir. Be patient. Gradually, the mystery, the unique identity, of the object or scene will unfold before your eyes. As you become more accustomed to this way of viewing Lilias's works, so will you begin to see the beauties of your own surrounding world reveal themselves. And then the purpose for which this little volume was created will be fulfilled.

Before you embark on this voyage of discovery, a few bits of background and biographical information are in order. You will be looking at scenes from a variety of places where Lilias lived and journeyed, from the English countryside to the deserts of North Africa, from perilous mountain passes to scenes of everyday life in the Casbah of Algiers. To all these vistas she brought a fresh and eager eye, but also an unerring gift for capturing vast expanses in the smallest compass. Living the life of a missionary in rugged terrain, Lilias did not have the luxury of large canvases and boxes of paints and brushes with which to work. She captured these impressions "on the fly," using a bare minimum of equipment—a small brush or pencil, a few paints, and a tiny four-by-six sketchbook or two-inch square space in the margin of a journal for canvas. Some of the images you will see in this book—scenes of a glorious desert sunset, of a large bay, of a sunrise on the sea—will have been created on a surface no larger than a matchbook. Conversely, she could fill up that small space with a single image of a seed pod or a bee fumbling among flower blossoms, and you would swear that you are seeing a much larger surface—a canvas of, say thirty-six by twenty-four inches. Very few artists have this capacity for elegantly rendering vast spaces in a tiny compass, or depicting a seemingly insignificant thing—a shell, a puppy, or clump of grass—as if it were the subject of a large and major work. Rembrandt and Dürer come to mind, but very few others. Lilias Trotter is one of those very few.

This faculty of accurately interpreting space, of attending with equal care and attention to the very large and the very small, was also emblematic of her approach to people. Each person, no matter how destitute, dirty, and downtrodden, was a precious soul, a being who bore within him- or herself the image of God. Just as the fumbling bee could be as worthy a subject of painting as a distant view of a vast mountain range, so was a six-year-old Muslim child as worthy of attention as a powerful London banker.

Lilias Trotter renounced a potentially glorious career as an artist in order to work as a missionary in North Africa, a calling both difficult and fraught with peril for a young woman of frail health from London's upper middle class. The great critic John Ruskin said "she would be the greatest living painter and do things that would be Immortal"—but only on condition that she give herself up entirely to art. This she would not do, but the images in this little book reveal how she continued to use her artistic gift, even though art was no longer the main focus of her life. Rather like her contemporary Gerard Manley Hopkins, whose exquisite poetry came to light only after his death, and who often felt his life as a priest in God's service bore little fruit, Lilias's art was hidden for long years, and her toil in the deserts of North Africa seemed to meet with limited success. But Hopkins and Trotter have now both been brought back from obscurity into the light, and both artists in their respective domains are inspiring new ways of seeing, new ways of appreciating God's magnificent, infinitely varied, wonderfully curious creation. As Hopkins said,

> And for all this, nature is never spent;
> There lives the dearest freshness deep down things...

It is those things and more that await you, as you learn to practice a new Way of Seeing.

—*Darcy Weir*
Classics Scholar; Lecturer on Art and Faith

*Finally, brothers and sisters, whatever is true, whatever is noble, whatever
is right, whatever is pure, whatever is lovely, whatever is admirable—if anything
is excellent or praiseworthy—think about such things.*

Philippians 4:8 (NIV)

Believe in the darkness what you have seen in the light.

1 August 1921

With God—these are the wonderful words,
this is the wonderful fact that changes
earth's sordid surroundings into the
heavenly places where we are seated with God.

The Letter "M"

El Kahtara

(women)

Life is grandly simple when the spirit of calculating results
and consequences, even spiritual results and consequences,
has been left among the things that are behind,
when obedience is the one thing that matters, when God Himself,
and no mere "experience" is our exceeding great reward.

A Ripened Life

Let faith swing out on Him.

He is the God of the impossible.

The Glory of the Impossible

The stretched-out hand of faith on earth,
acting in union with the stretched-out hand
of God's power in heaven.
That is the sort of faith
we have got to learn before we have done with it.

1 January 1900

He didn't promise us ease and comfort—
but He did promise joy which we may have
in the midst of any weight or heaviness
that may be ours to bear.

17 July 1920

The daisies have been talking again—
the reason they spread out their leaves flat on the ground
is because the flowers stretch out their little hands, as it were,
to keep back the blades of grass
that would shut out the sunlight.
They speak so of the need of deliberately holding back everything
that would crowd our souls
and stifle the freedom of God's light and air.

6 April 1899

He makes the scraps of aloneness very very precious—
one gets a sense among the palms and fruit blossoms
that one has so far as possible shut the door.
And it is true as of old that "the doors being shut, came Jesus."

3 March 1895

We love to see the impossible done. And so does God.

The Glory of the Impossible

Nettle !

We have to do with One who "inhabiteth eternity"
and works in its infinite leisure.

Parables of the Christ-Life

And it has come to me with a flood of joy
that no matter if we are only crooked little chinks,
the heavenly Sun can send through us not only light,
but the revelation of His Image:
"the light of the knowledge of the glory of God
in the Face of Jesus."

4 June 1900

"In truth the Spirits
are in it"

The things that are impossible with men are possible with God.
May it not be that the human impossibility
is just the very thing that set His Hand free?
And that it is the things which are possible for us to do
that He is in a measure to let alone?

22 May 1899

The still pool of living water lies in every saved soul,
keeping life within that little plot of ground,
but there is a world of difference between a pool and a river.
A river is wide open to its source
and as wide open to the needs lower down.
We need all barriers down—manward as well as Godward—
to believe for the outflowing as definitely as the inflowing.

3 August 1895

Oh, the desert is lovely in its restfulness.
The great brooding stillness over and through everything
is so full of God.
One does not wonder that He used to take His people
out into the wilderness to teach them.

6 March 1895

For the world's salvation was not wrought out
by the three years in which He went about doing good,
but in the three hours of darkness
in which He hung, stripped and nailed,
in uttermost exhaustion of spirit, soul, and body—till His heart broke.
So little wonder for us if the price of power is weakness.

27 October 1924

The growing point of our soul
is the thing with which the Spirit of God
is especially dealing with
and all depends on faithfulness there.

23 September 1902

Ain Touta flowers.

wild Artichoke

God's guidance, if our soul's instinct is healthy,
tallies with the sense of rest.

30 September 1903

June 19 - 1889

Holiness, not safety, is the end of our calling.

Parables of the Cross

I am seeing more and more
that we begin to learn what it is to walk by faith
when we learn to spread out all that is against us:
—all our physical weakness, loss of mental power, spiritual inability
all that is against us inwardly and outwardly—
as sails to the wind
and expect them to be vehicles
for the power of Christ to rest upon us.
It is so simple and self-evident—
but so long in the learning!

22 August 1902

God wants to show us that nothing
is great or small to Him.

26 March 1924

Blida.

We are proving these days that time is nothing to God:
nothing in its speeding, nothing in its halting.
He is the God that "inhabiteth eternity."

12 December 1920

Such a day of small things still,
but on God's time, and that is enough:
size as well as time and space count nothing with Him.

1 January 1902

The baby new moon was hanging in the sunset tonight
like a boat for the little angels . . .

11 February 1899

All the more beautiful will be God's triumph when it comes.
The highest music is not the music
where all goes on simple and straight and sweet,
but where discord suddenly resolves tensions with harmony.

12 February 1905

A flower that stops short of its flowering misses its purpose.

We were created for more than our own spiritual development;

reproduction not mere development,

is the goal of matured being—

reproduction in other lives.

Parables of the Cross

The history of His wonders in the past
is a constant succession of new things
and He is not at the end of His resources yet.

The Glory of the Impossible

God only knows the endless possibilities
that lie enfolded in each of us.

Parables of the Cross

If we can listen in stillness,
till our hearts begin to vibrate
to the thing He is thinking and feeling
about the matter in question,
whether it concerns ourselves or others,
we can from that moment
begin praying downwards from His throne,
instead of praying upwards to Him.

20 March 1926

You can never tell to what untold glories
any little humble path may lead,
if you only follow far enough.

13 August 1899

From near
Villa

Are our hands off the very blossom of our life?
Are all things—even the treasures that He has sanctified—
held loosely, ready to be parted with, without a struggle,
when He asks for them?

Parables of the Cross

Take the very hardest thing in your life
the place of difficulty, outward or inward,
and expect God to triumph gloriously in that very spot.
Just there He can bring your soul into blossom.

Parables of the Cross

The morning star is so perfectly marvelous these days.
It hangs in the dawn like a great globe of silver fire.
Of all the images of Christ
it seems the one that is almost more than an image—
it is so utterly like Him in its pure glory.

17 January 1899

There is a vibrating power
going on down in the darkness and dust of this world
that can make itself visible in starting results
in the upper air and sunlight of the invisible.
Each prayer beat here vibrates up to the very throne of God,
and does its work through that throne
on the principalities and powers around us . . .
We can never tell which prayer will liberate the answer,
but we can tell each one will do its work.

Vibrations

Vibrations

I have been thinking lately
what a work for God it is just loving people.

25 April 1891

The beginning of barley harvest

Hanging out clothes to dry!

(Time is not money)

Biskra People.

You are right to be glad in His April days
while He gives them.
Every stage of the heavenly growth is lovely to Him;
He is the God of the daisies
and the lambs
and the merry child hearts!

Parables of the Cross

There is a great sense of rest
in being in the way of His steps.

7 March 1915

When God delays in fulfilling our little thoughts,
it is to have Himself room to work out His great ones.

29 December 1903

Noiseless must be His Holy Habitation within us.

30 June 1895

The same lesson is reiterated all round by God:
the simple ABC lesson
that inadequacy and inefficiency on the human side
are His conditions for working.
"He sealeth up the hand of every man,
that all men may know His work."

27 February 1904

The milky-looking glacier torrent
spoke with God's voice this morning—
so obedient to its course in its narrow bed,
yet just tossing with freedom and swing in every motion.
Such a picture of the "rivers of living water"—
bound and yet unbound.

8 August 1899

The beauty of that old line of Hebrew poetry
came afresh today.
The thickest of the cloud storm
would be just where He is passing.
We see the dust now.
We shall see His Footprints
when He has passed along the way.

17 August 1919; 20 September 1924

In all the outward withholdings of this year,

God, as is His wont,

has been "opening" a door where He closes a window.

6 May 1904

We have to do with a God
to whom time is as boundless as space in its elasticity!

2 May 1914

Have you ever seen a shipyard?
The props were well and good while the boat was building,
but when the day has come for launching,
the props become hindrances instead of helps.
So down they must go to the very last one.
Then without an effort,
just by the weight of its own helplessness,
the ship takes its way to the sea.
Shall we gladly, and together, see the last props
of "someone" and "somehow" knocked away,
and swing off to the new venture
unsupported on the human side.
"My help cometh from the Lord
who hath made heaven and earth."

7 March 1928

Lago Maggiore

RELATED RESOURCES

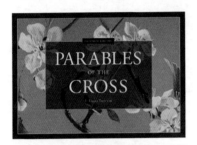

FACSIMILE EDITION

Parables of the Cross

BY LILIAS TROTTER

AVAILABLE ON AMAZON

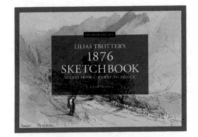

FACSIMILE EDITION

Lilias Trotter's 1876 Sketchbook: Scenes from Lucerne to Venice

ORIGINAL UNPUBLISHED ARTWORK BY LILIAS TROTTER

AVAILABLE ON AMAZON

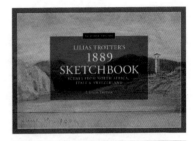

FACSIMILE EDITION

Lilias Trotter's 1889 Pocket Sketchbook: Scenes of North Africa, Italy and Switzerland

ORIGINAL UNPUBLISHED ARTWORK BY LILIAS TROTTER

AVAILABLE ON AMAZON

Lily: The Girl Who Could See

A CHILDREN'S BOOK BY SALLY OXLEY
& TIM LADWIG WITH MIRIAM HUFFMAN
ROCKNESS

AVAILABLE ON AMAZON

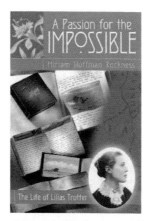

A Passion for the Impossible: The Life of Lilias Trotter.

BY MIRIAM HUFFMAN ROCKNESS
Published by Discovery House Publishers

A Blossom in the Desert: Reflections of Faith in the Art and Writings of Lilias Trotter

BY MIRIAM HUFFMAN ROCKNESS
Published by Discovery House Publishers

MANY BEAUTIFUL THINGS

THE LIFE AND VISION OF LILIAS TROTTER

WATCH THE FEATURE-LENGTH DOCUMENTARY EXPLORING THE LIFE OF LILIAS TROTTER

Watch the trailer

ManyBeautifulThings.com

Explore & learn about Lilias Trotter

liliastrotter.com

A documentary by award-winning filmmaker
LAURA WATERS HINSON
Featuring MICHELLE DOCKERY of DOWNTON ABBEY
as the voice of LILIAS TROTTER

Word of mouth is crucial for any author to succeed. If you enjoyed the book, please consider leaving a review where you purchased it, or on Goodreads, even if it's only a line or two; it would make all the difference and would be very much appreciated. You can also follow us on Twitter or "like" our page on Facebook. Thank you.

SAY HELLO!

WEBSITES	liliastrotter.com ManyBeautifulThings.com
	oxvisionmedia.com oxvisionfilms.com
TWITTER	@OxvisionFilms @OxvisionMedia
FACEBOOK	facebook.com/oxvisionfilms facebook.com/oxvisionmedia
	facebook.com/ManyBeautifulThingsMovie
EMAIL	info@liliastrotter.com

JOIN OUR NEW RELEASES EMAIL LIST

oxvisionfilms.com

BE THE FIRST TO HEAR ABOUT
NEW RELEASES FROM OXVISION FILMS

We promise not to share your email with
anyone else, and we won't clutter your inbox.
You can unsubscribe at any time.

Made in the USA
Charleston, SC
04 September 2016